Sales Made Easy For Entrepreneurs

PITCH PRODUCTS & SURVIVE,

SELL VALUE & THRIVE

Robert Kinch and Frank Dion

Get More Sales Corporation, 23-1111 Suite 453 Davis Drive, Newmarket, Ontario, L3Y 9E5

Or send an email to sales@getmoresalescorp.com

FIRST EDITION

ISBN: 978-1-7770807-0-9

TESTIMONIALS

"... ROB AND FRANK WERE ABLE TO HELP SIMPLIFY OUR CORE VALUE PROGRAM INTO A VERY CLEAR AND CONCISE MESSAGE THAT TURNS THE SALES PROCESS INTO A NATURAL BUSINESS DISCUSSION."

Michael Macaro, Director Business Development, MCC

"THIS WAS NOT JUST SALES TRAINING, WE ACTUALLY DEVELOPED THE UNDERSTANDING OF OUR TRUE VALUE TO OUR CLIENTS AND NOW WE CAN ARTICULATE IT IN ONE SIMPLE STATEMENT"

Sam D'Aurizio, Managing Principle, Solutia SDO

"GET MORE SALES PROVIDED US A PRACTICAL STEP BY STEP APPROACH TO DETERMINE OUR GROWTH STRATEGY AND THE "HOW TO" APPROACH OF SALES CONVERSATION FOR AGRILUX™ LIGHTING SYSTEMS ".

Alex Thies, President, Thies Electrical Distributing Ltd

"EXCELLENT ... AND THE NEW VALUE PROPOSITION WILL HELP ME SECURE MORE CLIENTS AND PARTNERS. OUR NEW PROPOSITION WILL HELP ME SPEND QUALITY TIME WITH SERIOUS BUYERS AND STOP WASTING TIME WITH THE NON-SERIOUS."

"I LEARNED HOW TO PROPERLY AND EFFECTIVELY PITCH OUR COMPANY. THIS WILL HELP ME CONNECT BETTER WITH POTENTIAL CLIENTS AND GAUGE THEIR INTEREST BEFORE I ENGAGE."

CONTENTS

INTRODUCTION

FOR ENTREPRENEURS

This book is for you the entrepreneur. You have built your business around a brilliant idea. A genius in your field, you have leveraged your network to drive success. Now, having run out of your network, you've hit the revenue ceiling. You are used to doing everything, but for some reason sales is a blind spot for you and you now have seen your growth slow down. This is a frustrating place to be and you may be wondering how to turn this situation around.

WHAT'S IN IT FOR YOU

This book is for you. If you are an entrepreneur that is challenged with selling and perceive it as a necessary evil and know you must do it but don't understand how, we will take the mystery out of it. We have a saying:

"SALES IS A PROCESS, NOT A PERSON"

It means that sales are a result of specific process and method, and not from hiring a person. We will teach you the method.

PITCH PRODUCT & SURVIVE,

SELL VALUE & THRIVE

Most entrepreneurs believe that if they tell everyone they meet about their product, they will make sales. Unfortunately, this only works temporarily. To really grow your business, you must start selling your value. Our process has helped many entrepreneurs get the knowledge, skills, plus implement order, structure, discipline, get control and the confidence to drive excellent predictable revenue growth. Follow it to grow your revenue & margin.

WHO ARE WE?

We have spent many years leading sales organizations in the fortune 500. We were privileged to have been trained in sales by IBM, Xerox, and other fortune 100 companies. It wasn't until we left these great companies, did we understand what we had our hands on.

We became entrepreneurs. We learned that without revenue coming in, we couldn't pay the bills. We had to build our solution and sell it. We were used to selling, but this time there was no salary to support us. It was commission only. Only then did we realize that we had learned something from all that fortune 100 experience - the value of a sales process. We could only fly by the seat of our pants for so long and were forced to build systems and sales process.

There are many gurus in sales that teach sales process and techniques. We were trained in most of them. For us sales guys, they made sense and seemed like common sense, but for a novice they seemed complicated. We didn't like that. Sales shouldn't appear so complicated because it isn't.

So, we came up with the idea for this book, Sales made Easy for Entrepreneurs. When we looked back at how we approached sales, we felt that it wasn't complicated. We believe sales is simply the art and science of successful conversations. Eighty percent of it is science, and twenty percent is art. The art is knowing when to apply the science. In this book you will find that once you understand a few foundational principles, you will be able to sell your wares simply and easily.

WHAT'S YOUR EXPERIENCE WITH SALES?

THE USED CAR GUY

What is your experience with sales people? When you hear the word sales, do you picture the "Used car sales guy". We totally understand why. Most of us remember negative far more than the positive experiences and all it takes is one negative sales experience to create a dislike for sales people.

So, what is your experience?

- Someone trying to sell you something you don't want?

- A sales person that keeps talking… and talking… and talking… until your eyes glaze over!

- Maybe you've experienced the pushy sales rep that doesn't take no for an answer.

- You've asked them a question, and they answer you with something completely irrelevant making you wonder if they've even listened to you.

- What about that slimy feeling you get when you have bought something because you felt pressured into buying it.

- Finally, perhaps you feel the hesitation because you really don't **TRUST** the sales guy.

Unfortunately, this is most entrepreneurs' impression of sales people. They associate this experience with sales.

Well, we are here to tell you, **THIS IS NOT SALES**. We hope by the time you have finished this book, you will agree.

THE BUYER'S JOURNEY

The first step to understanding sales is to recognize that every person that buys something goes through the buyer's journey. We believe this journey applies in almost all situations. Every sale starts with value. Buyers must perceive that your product or service meets their needs and they must see enough value in it to give you money. We will be walking through this journey throughout this book. This is what their journey looks like:

- Value messaging creates CURIOSITY
- Curiosity prompts BUYING SIGNALS
- Buying signals begin the SALES CONVERSATION
- The Sales conversation uncovers URGENCY
- Urgency triggers EMOTION
- Emotion is justified by LOGIC
- Logic secures the ORDER

CURIOSITY

How you tell the world about your product or service, will cause them to engage or be totally disinterested. Are you telling them about the value they will receive if they buy your product? A properly defined value message will create a glimpse of why they should buy your product. This "glimpse" creates curiosity in the buyer and causes them to engage.

BUYING SIGNALS

A curious prospect will engage you in some level of conversation. This engagement is a buying signal. Once you get the buying signal, they are ready to talk to you about your product.

THE SALES CONVERSATION

The buying signal opens the door to the sales conversation. Realize that the sales conversation is just that – a conversation. It is not manipulative, nor is it phony. You must ask questions and make statements as you would in any conversation. The only difference is the end goal of your sales conversation is to uncover urgency.

URGENCY

The goal of your sales conversation is to uncover the urgency of the buyer's issues. If there is no urgency in the buyer, then they will not buy from you. Urgency is key to making any sale. It works because it creates emotion.

EMOTION

When we sell, we sell to people and people are emotional beings. It is this emotional reaction, caused by issues in their business, that caused them to engage with you in the first place. If the emotion is strong enough to create urgency, you are more likely to make a sale as long as you can justify your solution with logic.

LOGIC

All buyers must at some point prove to themselves that your product or service makes sense for them. This justification comes in the form of validation from any variety of sources: customer testimonials, academic validation, or most importantly monetary return on their investment. Only then, will you get an **ORDER**.

We will be digging deeper into each of these concepts through the rest of this book. They are not difficult to learn, and when you study them, you will find out that sales isn't that hard. So, let's get started.

SELLING IS ABOUT TRUST

Trust is the prime ingredient in any sale. In today's society, because of the pervasiveness of the internet, social media and the like, we are guilty until proven innocent. This has made sales more challenging. We now must earn trust immediately. So how do you do it? Well, in this book, we will show you how to build trust with a potential buyer of your offering and how that trust will make them willing to give you money. It's actually not that hard. You just need the formula.

The following chart illustrates the buyers mindset as you go through the sale:

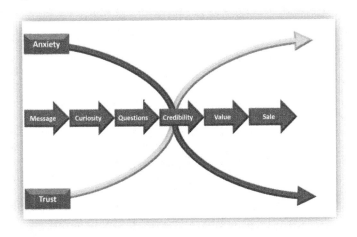

THE TRUST CURVE

The potential buyer begins in a state of anxiety. They are typically skeptical and are unsure and unwilling to speak with you. You have to earn their trust and earn the right to move with them through the sales cycle. As you do, they will begin to trust you more, and when they trust you more than they doubt you, they will purchase from you. This is the Trust curve.

The steps we use to move the prospect through this curve are simply a series of successful conversations. Each conversation establishes your credibility, earns their trust, and moves you closer to the sale. Finallly when they trust in the value that you offer, you close the sale. This is how you progress through the trust curve to a sale.

DEVELOPING TRUST

Our first rule in sales is:

You can't sell something to anyone until they give you permission to sell to them!

This is the first key to building trust. So how do you get permission from the prospect(buyer)? You must have a message that makes them curious about what you have to offer. So how do you do that? Well, you must condense your entire business into a single, concise, phrase that presents your value in 10 seconds or less. This phrase will create curiosity in the buyer, causes them to engage with you, and starts the buyers journey.

This is the foundation of conversation, any conversation. People, in general, will not engage with you in a conversation, unless they are curious about what you have to say. The way to create curiosity is to provide them **"Glimpses of Value"** that are specific to them. These glimpses come from your message. Your message is a simple 10 second statement that condenses the value you provide. The "value" is presented as sales triggers in your statement and sales triggers create curiosity. The result – you get a buying signal from serious prospects.

THE TRUST MINDSET

There is a nuance to our entire approach. We call this the **"Trust Mindset"**. It is simply a sincere, honest, approach to helping the prospect. A willingness to walk away if you can't help them. In other words, good sales people do not have tricks. They are not manipulative. They are truly customer focused, and want to help.

The process that we will outline, if you follow it, will in itself provide the **trust mindset.**

Key Points

YOU CAN'T SELL SOMETHING TO ANYONE UNTIL THEY GIVE YOU PERMISSION

DEVELOP A TRUST MINDSET TO BE SUCCESSFUL

CREATE YOUR VALUE MESSAGE

WHAT IS VALUE?

The truth is, people don't care about you or your product. They care about what's in it for them. If your customers are consumers, or businesses, they look for the same thing – value. Let us illustrate.

- Why do you buy a power drill? Why do you buy a drill bit? Is it to own either of these? The answer is, you want a hole. They are just tools to get you the hole.

- Why do businesses buy your software? To improve their business.

- Why do businesses buy your services? To improve their bottom line.

Our definition of value, in the business sense, is as follows: how do you help them make more money, or save on costs? If your customer is a consumer, value can be defined more personally, but the principle is still the same. Value is the perceived benefit of what you do regardless of how you do it.

SELL WHAT THEY WANT

To determine the value you provide, you must step out of your box, and put yourself in your prospects box. What do they think is valuable and NOT what YOU think is valuable? This is the biggest mistake we see entrepreneurs make. They tout all the features of their product, boring the prospect and pushing them away. Thinking they are focusing on value, they are simply regurgitating their features in a way that sounds like value. They are simply pitching their products.

THE VALUE MESSAGE

Your value message condenses the benefits your product or service into a concise 10 second statement that creates curiosity in the prospect. It is created based on the prospect's perceived value of your solution. The result of doing this properly is a concise message that causes the prospect to respond to you. They can key on specific points in your statement and are interested in discussing them with you.

How do you create this 10 second, concise message that summarizes what your business does, creates curiosity, and causes prospects to engage with you? You must start looking at your solutions from your prospect's perspective. Here are a few questions you can ask yourself to get your started.

Why do your customers buy from you?

- Talk to some existing customers; ask them the business value they received from your offering.

- Think of some recent customer successes and ask, how did their business improve because of our offering

---

What makes you unique in the marketplace (from your customers perspective)?

- Do you understand what advantages you have over your competition?

- What value do these advantages provide to your customer? In other words, what's in it for them?

CREATING YOUR MESSAGE

Now it is time to create your value message. This exercise may take some time. Don't rush it.

1. Write down all the benefits you perceive as valuable to your customers' business

2. Prioritize the benefits to identify the most important

3. Categorize the benefits

4. Build your message.

Here are some examples of this approach in action. We have provided the before and after for you:

Before	After
A new revolutionary LED spectrum light bulb Solution Poultry LED spectrum Lighting	**VALUE MESSAGE** A tailor-made lighting system that improves poultry production while lowering your operating costs
We produce tablets and retail systems for hospitality that allow you to connect with your employees and give them access to the internet while at work.	**VALUE MESSAGE** We create efficiencies that improve your customer and employee experience.

This message has many names: Message, Elevator Pitch, Single Overriding Communications Objective (SOCO) or General Benefits Statement. We like to call it your **VALUE MESSAGE**.

When done right, your message will create curiosity in the prospects mind, and stimulate interest in what YOU have to offer. It works because we are keying on what they care about, not what you care about. It creates the foundation of the sales conversation.

Key Points

SELL YOUR VALUE NOT YOUR PRODUCT

KNOW HOW TO ARTICULATE YOUR VALUE CONCISELY IN UNDER 10 SECONDS

SALES TRIGGERS

WHAT IS A SALES TRIGGER?

A sales trigger is a word or phrase in your message that causes the prospect to engage with what you are saying. Sales triggers are the doors to curiosity and are the keys that unlock the door to begin the sales conversation, and they provide glimpses of value into what you can provide to the prospect.

For example, when someone asks you what you do, you simply reply:

I am with XXXX, we

create efficiencies (Sales Trigger 1)

that

improve your customer (Sales Trigger 2)

and

employee experience (Sales Trigger 3)

You are looking for the prospect to connect with your sales triggers. If they do, then it means you have made a statement about something they are potentially interested in. If they don't, then you can move on to someone else. Don't spend time with someone that is never going to buy from you. Woah.... Did we just tell you to walk away from prospects? Absolutely! You see, the number one reason entrepreneurs have trouble closing deals, is that they are trying to sell to people that are never going to buy from them. It is just as important that the sales triggers in your message dissuade prospects from engaging with you as it is to persuade them to engage with you.

SALES TRIGGERS CREATE BUYING SIGNALS

What is a buying signal?

A buying signal from a prospect is simply a sign of interest in your message. Remember our key point from Chapter 2:

You can't sell something to anyone until they give you permission!

When someone gives you a buying signal, they are opening the door to a conversation. You must engage in that conversation by recognizing the buying signal. So, what does a buying signal look like? Here are a few examples:

- How do you do that?
- I have done that before and it didn't work!

- That sounds interesting, tell me more!

What most entrepreneurs (people attempting to sell) do is start talking as soon as they hear these "buying signals" from a prospect. The launch into their product pitch. This is a big mistake that kills sales. You see, you can't really respond yet, and you don't want to. The key to sales triggers creating buying signals is that they open doors that give you permission to sell. The prospect opens the door by responding to your value. When the door opens, it is important you don't immediately walk through it. When the prospect connects with the sales triggers in your statement, they are saying to you, "I am open to having a conversation about your value, but I'm not sure how you can help me". So how should you respond to the *buying signal?*

READ BETWEEN THE LINES

Before you respond to the buying signal, you must read between the lines. What do we mean? Well, let's take one of the example statements above.

Prospect: *"I've done that before, it didn't work!"*

You have to "guess" at what is really going on in the mind of this prospect. Why are they responding this way to our message? You must read between the lines. The buying signal is signaling something going on in their business and you must figure out what it is. Here is what we mean:

When they make this statement, it could mean the following:

- They bought the competition, and the project failed.

- They have tried to create a homegrown solution to the problem and couldn't get it done.

- They have had the problem in their business before.

You must make an educated guess to understand their situation. There is a great quote from the book by Stephen Covey, 7 habits of Highly Effective People. It is Habit #5:

Seek first to understand, then to be understood.
(Covey)

QUESTIONS REVEAL THEIR STORY

You can't respond to their buying signal because you don't know enough about their situation. So, how do you start to understand their situation? You ask questions! You must clarify the buying signal that they have given you. When you ask questions, you control the conversation not the prospect. Questions also cause the prospect to start thinking about their own situation. Finally, the questions you ask and the responses to them will reveal whether you can help the prospect or not.

Here is how a typical sales conversation might look:

Mary is the VP Sales at Acme Hospitality solutions and she meets Bob at a networking event. Bob is the COO of Pleasure

Cruise Lines.

> **Bob:** *Mary, so what do you do?*
>
> **Mary:** *Well Bob, I'm with Acme hospitality solutions Inc., We create efficiencies that improve your customer and employee experience.*
>
> **Bob:** *You know, we have tried to do that, and it didn't work.*

(Reading Between the lines **Mary** guesses: did they do it themselves? They didn't have the skill? They didn't get efficiency?)

> **Mary:** *Bob, when you say it didn't work, do you mean you created a solution for your employees to make them more efficient, and it didn't work?*
>
> **Bob:** *Yes.*
>
> **Mary:** *How so?*
>
> **Bob:** *We built something in-house, to allow them to communicate with their families while on our ships, and we ran into all sorts of cost overruns. We had to shut it down.*

Hopefully you can see in this conversation, Mary doesn't jump in and tell Bob, everything they do. She must first clarify

Bob's statement to answer correctly, if she can answer at all. After all, she may not be able to help him. Remember our selling mindset, if we can't help, we won't help.

In this example, Mary simple responds to Bob's statement with a question. The question is based on an educated guess because she was reading between the lines. That question revealed to her that they have tried something but did it themselves. She now knows more about why Bob connected with her message.

So why does this work? There is a basic human trait that forms the foundation of having a successful sales conversation – Curiosity. It opens the door to the conversation.

Key Points

SALES TRIGGERS CREATE BUYING SIGNALS

ALWAYS READ BETWEEN THE LINES

STOP TALKING AND ASK QUESTIONS

MAKE SURE YOU CONTROL THE CONVERSATION

CREATE CURIOSITY

WHAT IS CURIOSITY?

The official Webster dictionary definition of "Curiosity" is: interest leading to inquiry. In other words, if someone is curious about something you said, they have interest in your statement and will ask you about it. They want to know more about what you have to say. This human trait will cause people to be interested in a variety of things. Here are some examples:

- You hear a noise in your house that makes you curious about what made the noise and causes you to investigate.

- Someone mentions your name across the room, and now you are wondering what they said about you.

- Someone mentions a topic, like improving your bottom line, and now you want to know how they do that.

THE ROLE OF CURIOSITY IN SELLING

As we have already mentioned, Sales triggers create curiosity. Why? They present glimpses of value to the prospect. What does the prospect find valuable? Hopefully, your offering.

GLIMPSES OF VALUE

What do we mean by "Glimpses of Value"? A glimpse is a momentary or partial view of something. We have all had this experience. Have you ever seen something out of the corner of our eye? Have you noticed something in the distance and struggled to see it clearly? Each of these examples cause us to do something more, to engage. Once we have had a glimpse of something, we are then curious enough to engage further in that something. Now we find ourselves searching for more about that something. This is the heart of curiosity.

So, to gain the interest of a prospect, you must present to them glimpses of value. Remember our first exercise of identifying what is valuable to our customers, and not us? We must identify this so that we can create "Sales triggers" based on that value. These sales triggers are just glimpses of something that they need or want. We then built them into our MESSAGE. Therefore, it is SO important to get your MESSAGE in place. It forms the foundation of your sales conversation.

PROSPECT MOTIVATORS

Before we talk about what to do with a curious prospect, we must understand what motivates people to act. There are three categories of key motivators (Freese, 2013) that cause prospects to engage: We call them: German Shepherds, Gold Medals, and Following the Herd.

GERMAN SHEPHERDS

Have you ever seen someone run away in fear from something? Was it a dog? Can you picture a person wearing a padded suit and a police dog, a German shepherd, attacking them? At that moment when they see the dog, what is motivating them? Aren't they afraid something bad is going to happen to them?

A "German Shepherd" motivator is a situation or event that drives a negative outcome to the individual experiencing it. It creates a negative emotion. In a sales environment, these could be: revenue is declining, compliance to government regulations, potential fines, or rising costs of doing business.

German Shepherds create the strongest motivation for a prospect to act. This is just human nature. We are all more likely to act if we are in fear or experiencing discomfort. They represent about 20% of the prospects you will encounter.

GOLD MEDALS

When you watch the Olympics, is your favorite part the medal ceremony? When you watch the medal being placed around the neck of your country's athlete do you get tears in your eyes? Do you Feel proud?

A "Gold Medal" motivator, unlike a German shepherd, is a situation or emotion that drives an Olympic level feeling of achievement in the individual experiencing it. It creates a positive emotion. Just as athletes are motivated to go through the struggle of training, failure, and injury to achieve the feeling of accomplishment as they stand on the podium, so do entrepreneurs of companies to be the first, the best, the biggest, the richest, or the greatest.

In a sales situation, these could be: Number one in customer satisfaction, awarded the best company to work for, or being the leader in the industry. The typical company that responds to the gold medal motivators are what the industry calls "early adopters".

Gold medals create strong motivation but aren't always urgent. They also only represent about 5% of the prospects you will uncover.

FOLLOWING THE HERD

Have you ever been on a farm and noticed that you never see just one cow standing alone in the pasture? Don't they almost always seem to be following a leader, or huddled together?

A "Follow the Herd" motivator is a situation that drives individuals to "keep up with their neighbor". They move to action because someone else, like them, is moving. Just as the cows in the field follow each other, so do people. They don't want to be first, and are concerned about being last, so they simply follow their peers. They do this because their tolerance for risk is low and they like to see that someone else, in their industry, is doing it.

This motivator represents about 75% of all prospects. It is the most effective way to create curiosity. If the prospect has the same problem as their peers, and you solved it for their peers, they will at least want to hear about it.

CURIOSITY AND THE SALES CONVERSATION

Every conversation starts with curiosity. As we mentioned, the sales triggers in your message provide glimpses of value which in turn create curiosity. It is curiosity that causes a prospect to engage with you. This is a buying signal. It is now up to you to know what to do with the buying signal.

Now that we know more, let's review the conversation Mary had with Bob. Here's how it went:

Bob: *Mary, so what do you do?*

Mary: *Well Bob, I'm with Acme hospitality solutions Inc., We create efficiencies that improve your customer and employee experience.*

Mary has used her message to see if she can get permission from Bob to have a sales conversation. Notice the sales triggers in Mary's message: Create Efficiencies, Improve your Customer and Employee Experience. The key to creating curiosity with this statement is to state the message, then... STOP TALKING. We have heard so many entrepreneurs make a statement and then never let the prospect answer or respond. You must have experienced this. This is what makes you sound like the used car sales guy. Luckily, Mary waited to see if Bob gave her a response. This is the key to creating curiosity with the statement. She gives time for Bob to respond. If Bob doesn't respond to her statement, then he is NOT CURIOUS, and she does not have permission to sell ANYTHING to him.

Bob: *You know, we have tried to do that, and it didn't work*

.

Bob has responded. As a matter of fact, Bob has revealed something very important to Mary in his response. He has the problem. It is now up to Mary to dig deeper and identify what happened. To do this, she must first make an educated guess as we stated previously. Reading Between the lines Mary guesses: Did they do it themselves? They didn't have the skill? They didn't get efficiency?

> **Mary:** *Bob, when you say it didn't work, do you mean you created a solution for your employees to make them more efficient, and it didn't work?*

Mary has decided to explore if they built the solution themselves.

> **Bob:** *Yes.*
>
> **Mary:** *How so?*
>
> **Bob:** *We built something in-house, to allow them to communicate while on our ships to their families, and we ran into all sorts of cost overruns. We had to shut it down.*

Now Mary continues the conversation and tries to uncover what motivated Bob's company to do what they did.

> **Mary:** *Why did you need them to communicate with their families? What made it so important to invest money in building a solution?*
>
> **Bob:** *Well, when your employees are at sea for 8 months,*

they tend to get homesick, and if they can't communicate to their families, they burn out and quit. This turnover was costing us millions.

Mary has uncovered the reason. A big German shepherd. It was costing them millions. So, what does she say next?

Key Points

CURIOSITY STIMULATES INTEREST

*GERMAN SHEPHERDS, GOLD MEDALS, AND
FOLLOWING THE HERD IS WHAT MOTIVATES
PROSPECTS*

SHUT UP AND LISTEN, ALWAYS!

BUILDING THE SALES CONVERSATION

WHAT IS A CONVERSATION?

Any conversation, whether you are at a backyard barbeque or a garden party, consists of a series of questions, statements, and responses. Recall the last time you were in a conversation with someone. Did you ask them some questions? Maybe you touted your expertise on a certain topic? Maybe you started arguing with them and they with you? These are all elements of a conversation.

There is, however, one thing that all of us do that inhibits a truly valuable interaction with someone. That is, we really don't care what they are saying, we simply want to talk about what we want to talk about. We don't really listen to them. Have you ever noticed that when someone says something to you in conversation, you are looking for places to interrupt them and insert your point of view on the topic? Then you get annoyed when they won't stop talking long enough for you to interject.

How about this one? They introduce themselves to you, tell you their name and thirty seconds into the conversation, you can't remember what they said their name was.

All this is fine, if you're just talking with people, but if you want to engage in sales, then these negative habits will kill you. You must learn to listen.

SUCCESSFUL CONVERSATIONS

WHAT IS A SUCCESSFUL CONVERSATION?

We have already defined what makes up a conversation, but what is a successful conversation? In sales, it is one that leads you to uncover the issues of your prospect and creates credibility, in their eyes, for you and your company. This credibility increases their level of trust in you and your company and that trust leads them to reveal urgent issues in their business. Those urgent issues create enough emotion for them to act and because they now trust you, they give you money.

It sounds complicated, but it isn't really. In simple terms, you simply listen and respond.

Listen

The number one skill in successful sales people is the ability to listen. If you become a great listener, you will dispel all the salesperson stereotypes. You will also create more relationships in general. We have a very simple 4-Step approach to making you a good listener.

STOP

- Don't interrupt the prospect.

- Don't jump into the conversation.

- Don't say anything until the prospect stops talking.

LISTEN

- Focus on the words they are speaking.

- Don't get distracted.

- Pay attention.

CLARIFY

- Restate what you think you heard. This sounds something like: "Let me see if I understood what you said...".

- Restate what you heard them say.

RE-CLARIFY

- Stay in the loop.

- Keep Clarifying and Restating until the prospect says, "yes, that's correct".

QUESTION

- Ask another question.

The key technique in the process is "CLARIFY". This

alone forces you to listen. If you must restate what you heard, then you must hear something. To "hear" something, you must listen. By stating what you heard, your prospect thinks: "Wow, they were actually listening!". Try it. It works.

Questions Create Credibility

We were recently evaluating our insurance policy. We had engaged a new agent but were a little unsure if she was the one we should use. Over a cup of coffee, she sat across the desk and started asking us questions. The questions were very interesting because they didn't appear to have anything to do with insurance. She didn't ask questions like, "How much insurance do you think you need?". She asked, "You're entrepreneurs. How many companies do you own?". "Are you concerned about your estates being taken by the tax man?". These are questions we never even thought of. Then she explained the benefits and unique ways we could use insurance inside the company. Here is what went through our heads. Wow, she seems to know what she is talking about because I never would have thought of that. We now viewed her as a CREDIBLE resource for our insurance needs.

You see, if she had simply stated, "I'm an expert in insuring business owners", we might have thought, "Yeah, right!". By asking us questions that forced us to think, questions that were relevant to us and our situation, we came to our own conclusion that she was a valuable resource that could fill in our knowledge gap. She became credible through her questions.

Questions are the key to establish value in the eyes of your prospects. They cause prospects to convince themselves. However, they must be planned and relevant.

Sales triggers and Questions

We must create questions that reveal our knowledge of the prospects situation but are strategic to our offering. The key to doing this are the sales triggers in our MESSAGE. Remember the sales triggers are key to our value, so if we focus on them in our questions, then we will be strategically leading the prospect toward our value.

Let's go back to the conversation between Mary and Bob. Mary's message is

---

We create efficiencies that improve your customer and employee experience

The sales triggers in Mary's message are "create efficiencies", "improve customer experience", and "improve employee experience". So, what are some questions Mary' should ask Bob in order to determine if she can help him. Here are some examples:

- What kind of experience were you trying to create for your employees?

- Why do you think it failed?

- Did you find that having to be "always on" when they were out of their quarters, contributed to the failure? How so?

- How did the poor employee experience impact the passenger experience?

- In our experience, cruise ship employees must be in uniform when in public, is that the case for your cruise line?

- What was the number one thing your employees are looking for?

By asking questions that illustrate her knowledge of Bob's business, Mary causes Bob to feel that she may have credibility and knowledge about the cruise line industry. He comes to the conclusion, himself, without Mary telling him.

Keep it a Natural Conversation

There is an old sales adage that says you should ask lots of questions and keep the prospect talking. Although this is partially true, it is not always true. You must have a balance of questions and statements. This is normal in any conversation. A true interaction involves revealing some of your knowledge and learning about the other person.

Have you ever been in a conversation with someone, and all they did was talk about themselves? How exciting was that? We're pretty sure that you got bored quickly. Likewise, when you are selling, if all you do is talk about what you know, your prospect will get bored and stop listening. So, you need to ask questions about them and their business.

Having said this, there is a fine line you don't want to step over when you ask questions.

Open and Closed Ended Questions

Closed ended questions are those which cause a **YES / NO** response.

Open ended questions are those which cause a **DETAILED** response.

The key to successful conversation is to mix and match closed and open-ended questions. If you only ask closed-ended questions, then the prospect will feel like you are interrogating them. The interrogation might look like this:

- How many users do you have? -- 12

- Do you turnover your employees? -- YES

- Do you have development staff? - YES

- How many staff do you have? – 15

Notice that you didn't get much information, and prospect is wondering where you are going with the questions and feeling a little attacked.

Open-ended questions should create detailed responses and provide much better insight into their situation. The prospect will also feel more "listened to". This type of question usually starts with a "Why" question. Here are some examples:

- What kind of experience were you trying to create for your employees?

- Why do you think it failed?

Do you notice the difference?

Statements

Statements in your conversation, when inserted properly, add to your credibility with the prospect. Statements are normal in any conversation. We make statements about topics that we have expertise in or are interested in regardless to whom we are talking.

A good conversation is a natural one that includes: closed-ended questions, open-ended questions, and statements.

Let's continue Mary and Bob's conversation:

Bob: *Mary, so what do you do?*

Mary: *Well Bob, I'm with Acme hospitality solutions Inc., We create efficiencies that improve your customer and employee experience.*

Bob: *You know, we have tried to do that, and it didn't work.*

(Reading Between the lines **Mary** guesses: did they do it themselves? They didn't have the skill? They didn't get efficiency?)

Mary: *Bob, when you say it didn't work, do you mean you created a solution for your employees to make them more efficient, and it didn't work?*

Bob: *Yes.*

Mary: *How so?*

Bob: *We built something in-house, to allow them to communicate while on our ships to their families, and we ran into all sorts of cost overruns. We had to shut it down.*

Mary: *Why did you need them to communicate with their families? What made it so important to invest money in building a solution?*

Bob: *Well, when your employees are at sea for 8 months, they tend to get homesick, and if they can't communicate to their families, they burn out and quit. This turnover was costing us millions.*

The conversation continues…

Mary: *How many employees were included in the solution?* **(close-ended)**

Bob: *3000.*

Mary: *What caused the cost overruns?* **(open-ended)**

Bob: *We had never done this before and quite frankly we didn't really know what we were doing, it was not our forte.*

Mary: *Well Bob, you know, we have built something similar for Gold Cruise lines and we were able to increase employee satisfaction by 80%.* **(Statement)**

Notice how Mary had used the key conversation elements, naturally to uncover the problem.

IDENTIFY NEED, UNCOVER URGENCY

In addition to the open-ended and close-ended questions, there are 3 categories of questions that we use to uncover the issues that will cause the prospect to buy from us. These are: Need, Urgency, and Budget.

Need Questions

These are questions that uncover the facts about the prospects situation and whether they have a problem. Every prospect has some form of need; however, this doesn't mean they are willing to act on them. To determine if they will act, we must establish or uncover their **urgency** around those needs.

We are all familiar with needs: "I need a new car", or "I need a new house.", or even "I need some new shoes." We have all made these statements, but do we act on them? When do we act on them? That depends on our motivators. For example, you may say, "I need a new car", but if your car is working and you are only 2 years into your payments on it, what is going to happen? You are unlikely to get a new car. Why? You don't have a german shepherd biting at your heals. It still runs and isn't costing you money, and you still owe a bunch of money on it.

What happens if you blow the engine? You buy a new car. Why? You must get to work, and you can't get there without the car. If you don't work, you can't pay the mortgage, and if you don't pay the mortgage, you become homeless. It has become **urgent** because the consequences of not buying the car, far out way the cost of the new car. So, even though you still have 3 years of payments on the old car, you figure out how to find the money for a new car.

In the above example, what has happened? You had something that you thought you needed, but your situation was comfortable, and it wasn't a priority to fix it. This resulted in you doing nothing about it. However, when an outside event changed your comfort level (the engine blew), your need became **urgent**. Only then were you willing to act on the need. You then figured out how to afford the need.

This is exactly what happens in sales. Your prospect goes through the same cycle. Have you ever had a conversation with a prospect, and they seemed very interested in buying your offering? They show all the signs of buying. You've given them pricing. You've talked to them and you know they need your offering. But for some reason, it has been 6 months, and you don't have an order. Here's why – there is NO URGENCY.

What is Urgency?

Urgency in the sales conversation is an event or situation that is causing the prospect to act now. It is what causes the prospect to give you money. Without it, your deals will not close.

Urgency is normally driven by internal forces in an organization, but it can sometimes be created by us. In all cases it is our role as entrepreneurs to uncover urgency and to ensure we develop it by asking questions about it with the prospect. Here are some examples of urgency.

- The HIPPA standard in the healthcare industry requires companies to comply with certain regulations. (German Shepherd)

- The Sarbanes Oxely act drives executives of publicly traded companies to explore information presented to them that could affect the business. (German Shepherd)

- A construction company has been accused of workplace safety violations and they must deal with it or loose their insurance. (German Shepherd)

- A startup has a goal of being number one in their industry and are spending without regard to profitability. (Gold Medal)

You will see that many of the situations or events that create urgency are German Shepherd motivators. We discussed these in chapter 4. This is because most of us, including companies, don't prioritize spending money unless there are negative consequences of not acting on the motivator. It is up to us, to ensure that the prospect is aware of the consequences, some they will know, and some they won't know about.

The diagram below illustrates the connection between Need, Urgency and Budget. We read it from the bottom up. A company / prospect will have many needs but not all of them are urgent. Only when they become urgent will they even consider creating a budget to solve them. So, as you can see, as we move up the pyramid, there are less "urgent needs" than there are needs, and even less "urgent needs" cause them to create a budget. In the conversation we must determine which needs are important enough for them to create a budget.

Notice that the least import issue in the needs pyramid is budget. Also notice that it doesn't come first. If you uncover a need that is urgent enough for the company to solve, then they will create a budget for it. Therefore, it is so important for us to establish urgency in the sales conversation.

CUSTOMER NEEDS PYRAMID

EMOTIONAL VS LOGICAL QUESTIONS

Emotional and logical questions are the next category of questions. If you are trying to create or uncover urgency, you must know the difference.

Emotional questions are just that, they stimulate some type of emotion in the prospect. They can be obvious or subtle. The value of this type of question, is this: We are emotional beings and,

---

We Make emotional decisions and justify them with logic.

Let us give you an example. Ladies... Shoes... need I say more. Ok, just to even it up, Men... Cars...

In business the same principle applies. Remember our motivators. What is more likely to create an emotional response? A German Shepherd or a Gold Medal. Usually it is a german shepherd. Why? German shepherds create negative **emotions** and almost all businesses prioritize negative influences because they typically have immediate impact on their bottom line. So, the more questions we can ask about a german shepherd motivator, the more likely we will reveal urgency. Each time we reveal the potential impact of a motivator, we create a reason for them to buy from us.

Logical questions help the prospect come to a conclusion.

We ask logical questions to illustrate matter of fact situations. They move the conversation from point A to point B. we have used these questions in Mary's conversation with Bob. For example, "how many employees were included?", or "What caused the cost overruns?". They are designed to pull information out of the prospect so that we can understand their situation better.

In the figure below, you can see how these questions are used to create emotional or logical responses in the prospect. Typically, urgency questions create emotional responses. Need questions can create emotional responses but not necessarily. And budget questions tend to be matter of fact questions. As a result, the dynamics of a sales conversation is a constant flow of need questions, statements, urgency questions, recognizing prospect motivators, and confirming if they plan to create a budget.

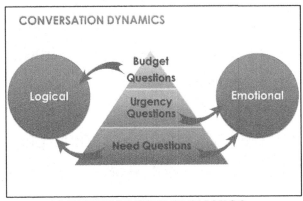

CONVERSATION DYNAMICS

IMPACT AND IMPLICATIONS

Emotional questions are used to reveal the impact of a motivator, and the implication it creates on the prospects business.

Remember our example of your car with the blown engine? This is an example of the power of implications of a motivator to drive urgency. The motivator in this case is the car blows its engine. The implications of this are: you must get to work and you can't get there without the car; if you don't work, you can't pay the mortgage; and if you don't pay the mortgage, you become homeless. Hopefully you can see that it is the implications that cause you to act.

In the sales conversation, we use emotional questions to draw out the implications of a situation. In our car example, a good car sales person would ask you:

- "So, if you don't buy a car today, what happens?"
- "If you can't drive to work, how will you get there? "

You can see how these two questions would get you thinking about the consequences of you not having a car. They make you think about the situation and begin to feel emotional about it.

THE CONVERSATIONAL STRUCTURE

Can you see how asking the right questions creates buy-in? When you are answering questions, you begin to convince yourself of your need and the urgency of your need. When you structure your conversation and your questions properly you will develop the need and determine the urgency of each need, and in the process the prospect will begin to feel the urgency. The greater the implications caused by the need, the more likely they will want to solve it.

To develop urgency properly, you must identify a need, and then develop that need to the determine the urgency. Don't jump around in the conversation. Stick to a single line of questioning until you have determined whether that need is urgent or not. Then move to the next need.

The Value Question

The value question tidies up the line of questioning. It presents the business value that you deliver to the prospect in a way that asks the prospect to confirm your value back to you. Here is how this may look with our car sales person:

- "If I could get you a car that fits within your budget that you could drive to work today, would that be of value to you? "

Notice that he didn't say, "would you buy today?". This would be manipulative. We want them to agree that it would be of value.

The Budget Question

Once the prospect agrees with the value you provide, it is now ok to ask about budget. There are ways to ask them about their budget without asking directly. We have found some prospects do not like to reveal their hand directly but will give you an idea of what it looks like. Here is an example:

- "Have you given any thought as to how much you would like to invest in this?"

- "Have you thought about how much this would cost?" What figure did you come up with?"

Let's go back to the conversation between Mary and Bob. Knowing what we know now, this is what it might look like.

Bob: *Mary, so what do you do?*

Mary: *Well Bob, I'm with Acme hospitality solutions Inc., We create efficiencies that improve your customer and employee experience.* **(MESSAGE)**

Bob: *You know, we have tried to do that, and it didn't work.* **(BUYING SIGNAL)**

(Reading Between the lines **Mary** guesses: did they do it themselves? They didn't have the skill? They didn't get efficiency?)

Mary: *Bob, when you say it didn't work, do you mean you created a solution for your employees to make them more efficient, and it didn't work?* **(CLARIFY)**

Bob: *Yes.*

Mary: *How so?* **(NEED QUESTION)**

Bob: *We built something in-house, to allow them to communicate while on our ships to their families, and we ran into all sorts of cost overruns. We had to shut it down.*

Mary: *Why did you need them to communicate with their families? What made it so important to invest money in building a solution?* **(CLARIFY THEN URGENCY)**

Bob: *Well, when your employees are at sea for 8 months, they tend to get homesick, and if they can't communicate to their families, they burn out and quit. This turnover was costing us millions.*

Mary: *How many employees were included in the solution?* **(close-ended) (NEED)**

Bob: *3000.*

Mary: *What caused the cost overruns?* **(open-ended) (NEED)**

Bob: *We had never done this before and quite frankly we didn't really know what we were doing, it was not our forte.*

Mary: *Wow that must have been frustrating for you.* **(EMOTION)**

Bob: *Yes, it drove me crazy. It was a big sore point for my division.*

Mary: *Did the problem go away once you shut the project down?* **(URGENCY)**

Bob: *No, the turnover is still as high as ever.*

Mary: *So, it's still costing you millions?* **(URGENCY)** *Is it still in the plan to solve it?* **(BUDGET)**

Bob: *Yes.... and why do you ask?*

Mary: *Well, I ask because we may be able to help you with that. What if you could have a solution in place in the next 90 days, would that be of value to you?* **(EMOTION)**

Bob: *I'm listening.*

Mary: *Well Bob, you know, we have built something similar for Gold Cruise lines and we were able to increase their employee satisfaction by 80%.* **(Follow the Herd)** *We built it in 90 days. Would it make sense to meet and discuss how we may be able to do the same for you?* **(Follow the Herd)**

Bob: *How does tomorrow at 10am sound?*

Mary: *I'll be there.*

This is an example of a sales conversation. As you can see, the conversation flows very naturally and as a result, Bob is willing to give us a meeting.

Key Points

HAVE A CONVERSATION

KNOW THEIR BUSINESS AND ASK CREDIBLE QUESTIONS

GET EMOTIONAL AND DEVELOP URGENCY, ALWAYS!

ORGANIZE YOUR SALES CYCLE

You have been able to create curiosity with your message, and you have asked strategic questions that established your credibility and earned you a meeting with the prospect. You have identified a need and established urgency. Now what do you do. You follow your established sales cycle.

WHAT IS A SALES CYCLE?

It is a series of logical steps that **YOU** define based on **YOUR** experience that lead the customer to decide to buy from you. We see many clients wandering aimlessly through the wilderness with clients unsure of where they are going. They have not defined the steps needed to earn the trust of the prospect and eventually earn an order. They allow the prospect to tell them what must happen next and as a result they lose control of the sale. The net result – they don't get orders. They typically talk to the prospect once or twice, give them a proposal or a quote and wait.

CONTROLLING THE SALES CYCLE

The first step to controlling **YOUR** sales cycle is map out your process. Your process starts at the first point of contact with a new lead (new prospective customer) and ends after you have cash in the bank. Each step in your process should have a purpose, and it should address some aspect of the prospects concerns. We believe that all sales cycles are circular because you should be generating business from your current customer as well as new one. At each stage in the sales cycle you are having a conversation to determine if it makes sense to proceed to the next step until you propose a solution to the prospect. The following is an example of a sales cycle:

SAMPLE SALES CYCLE

Each organization has its own version of this sales cycle. You will notice several elements that we like to include in the sales cycle for any company.

First, note the extra arrow we have placed between the two steps "Call Lead to Qualify" and the "Discovery Call". These two steps in the cycle can be two separate meetings or one meeting. The difference between the two are: in the "Call Lead to Qualify" step you are asking need and logical questions to determine if you can actually help the prospect (remember if you can't help them, don't continue), and in the "Discovery Call" step you are asking urgency and emotional questions to understand the situation and determine if they will act on the urgency.

Second, the Clarification Call is a step that most organizations miss. We have found that when we miss this step, the sale doesn't close. This step is in place because, even though we believe we have all the information we need to create a proposal, we must confirm our understanding once again with the prospect. Almost always, the prospect will add more to your understanding of their situation, but more importantly you are validating in their eyes, that you are listening to them. This is also a good opportunity to present a preliminary solution allowing you to test their acceptance of you and your solution prior to proposing, officially.

Third, note the "Demo" is only given to a prospect if

needed and it is done after the proposal and all discussion have occurred. We see far too many companies wasting time doing demos (another way to pitch your product) to prospects that will never buy from them. ***Demos should only be done to close the order, not to open the door.***

Finally, the 6-month follow up step is always required. It is far less expensive to get business from an existing customer than to find a new customer. Don't neglect your customers. They are a good source of business. Many of our clients do not stay connected with their current customers and have a follow up process to reach out to them regularly. This will impact customer retention and impact the bottom line.

MANAGING THE SALE

The Sales Cycle Email

The simplest way to manage this process with a prospect is to send them an email after the initial call outlining the steps you would like to take. Assign dates to each step including signing the order and ask the prospect to confirm they are ok with them. This forces the prospect to take the process seriously. If they confirm back to you the dates with the final "sign the proposal" date agreed to, then you have a real deal.

Here is what this might look like:

Dear (Bob the Exec),

Thank you for meeting with (Sponsor Name) and me earlier today. I believe it was time well spent for both (Prospect Company Name) and (Your Company Name). You confirmed that the following issues were important:(Issues – German Shepherds, Gold Medals).

- *(Issue 1)*
- *(Issue 2)*
- *(Issue 3)*

You said if you had the following Goals:

- *(Goal 1)*
- *(Goal 2)*
- *(Goal 3)*

You mentioned (Other titles and their resulting pains) that PERSON 1 and PERSON 2 had the same issue.

I am confident (Your Company Name) can provide these capabilities and pleased you want to commit the resources needed to evaluate our methodology. Based on my knowledge to date, I am suggesting that we take the following steps to ensure we deliver the right solution for you.

- *Meet with VP Marketing and discuss her needs (Date)*
- *Roundtable with technical users (Date)*
- *Clarify our findings and preliminary proposal (Date)*
- *Propose the solution (Date)*
- If needed, Proof of Concept or Demo (Date) (Billable event)
- Sign off on proposal (Date)

Please add any steps you feel are necessary. Let me know if I have missed anything.

Sincerely,

Mary Doe

Managing the sales cycle will save you time and money. Don't get caught wondering when your deals will close. Control the process.

Key Points

YOU CONTROL THE SALES CYCLE, NOT THE PROSPECT.

MANAGE THE STEPS - BOOK A MEETING FROM A MEETING (BAMFAM)

HANDLING OBJECTIONS

WHAT IS AN OBJECTION?

An objection is simply a buying signal that occurs during the sales cycle. However, they are a sign that you may have missed something in your conversation. Objections can arise for a variety of reasons. You may have missed a step in the sales cycle and because of it, the prospect isn't sold on your value. You could have failed to establish urgency in the prospects mind. In all cases we have a simple approach to handle them. We have already discussed the necessity of listening previously and laid out our listening process.

To handle objections instead of the last step in that process, "Ask another Question", we replace it with an "Answer". This is outlined below.

STOP

- Don't interrupt the prospect.

- Don't jump into the conversation.

- Don't say anything until the prospect stops talking.

LISTEN

- Focus on the words they are speaking.

- Don't get distracted.

- Pay attention.

CLARIFY

- Restate what you think you heard. This sounds something like: "Let me see if I understood what you said..." then restate what you heard them say.

RE-CLARIFY

- Stay in the loop.

- Keep Clarifying and Restating until the prospect says, "yes, that's correct".

ANSWER

- Answer the real question.

The key to handling objections properly is to recognize that the initial objection may not be the real objection. Here is what this may look like in Mary and Bob's conversation.

Bob: *Mary, the proposal price seems high?*

Mary: *What is it about the proposal that you find unreasonable?*

Bob: *We have been down this route before and I'm not sure I will get value for my money.*

Mary: *What do you mean "Been down this route before"?*

Bob: *Well we have done this ourselves.*

Mary: *Let me see if I understand what you are saying, you are concerned that we can't deliver on something that you have tried to build yourselves.*

Bob: *Yes, that's correct.*

Mary: *If you could speak to one of our current customers, would that make you feel comfortable enough to proceed?*

Bob: *Yes, I believe that would work.*

Notice that even though Bob initially brought up the price as an issue, the real issue was his confidence in spending the money on a solution that may not work. If Mary had simply responded to the objection by offering a lower price, she would still have a problem with closing the deal because that isn't what Bob is concerned about. He is concerned about her company's abilities. Mary must identify the real objection and make sure she addresses it. If she had simply dropped her price, as most companies do, she would have had difficulty closing the deal because price was not the objection.

Key Points

THE OBJECTION MAY NOT BE THE OBJECTION

STOP, LISTEN, CLARIFY, ANSWER!

A PROFESSION OF PROBABILITIES

Sales is a profession of probabilities. This makes it a unique profession that is very much misunderstood by the executives of a business. You see, most other areas of the business are very much based on defined inputs and defined outputs. The engineering department uses science and concrete values to create a new product. By adjusting the inputs, they can change the output. The end results are predictable based on the inputs.

In the sales function, this doesn't exist. We can only predict the probability of revenue, and can't guarantee revenue. Why? Unlike engineering, in sales we are dealing with people. In some cases many people are involved in a single sales decision. This makes it very difficult to predict the outcome. In addition, there are many outside forces that impact the decision of a prospect such as: other areas of the business, politics, or government regulations.

As a result, we have to manage sales based on probabilities. There are three components that drive probabilities in sales: Numbers, Stages, and Time.

NUMBERS

To accommodate for the fact that we can't control every variable in any one sale, we have to track many sales cycles. Another word for a prospect moving through the sales cycle is an opportunity. So in order to predict the amount of revenue that will be delivered by the sales team, we have to track the total revenue from all the opportunities. We need "numbers".

Start tracking the revenue as soon as you can estimate the value of the potential sale. Usually we have a general idea once an opportunity is at the "Validate Lead" stage (Remember our sales process). The farther the opportunity moves through your sales cycle, the more accurate the revenue prediction.

STAGES

Each step in the sales cycle is called a stage. We must understand and track the revenue at each stage of our sales cycle. At each stage in the sales cycle we are confirming the need and looking for urgency, which makes the opportunity more likely to close (Remember the trust curve). The more we prove our value to the prospect, the more likely they will buy from us. So as we move from sales stage to sales stage, we are more confident in the revenue.

TIME

Time is the most misunderstood part of sales. Many entrepreneurs build spreadsheets to lay out their 3 year cashflow for their busines. They treat this as a simply a financial exercise plugging in numbers looking for a result that "looks good". The problem with this approach is they are not allowing for time as a factor.

A typical sales cycle takes time to complete. In some cases it's 30 days and in some cases it's 1 year. You have to allow for this. Time plays an important role in forecasting revenue for your business and impacts your ability to predict revenue because you can simply run out of time.

REVENUE METRICS

We have a saying, "Know your Metrics". Here is what we mean by this. We have to leverage probabilities to determine the revenue that will close. To determine this, we need to know the revenue amount, the sales stage, and the time it takes to close an opportunity.

A probability is represented by a percentage value or a ratio. There are many revenue metrics that we track when managing the revenue for the business and if we covered all of them, you would be overwhelmed. However, we do recommend you at least track this one key revenue metric to get more consistent revenue. This revenue metric has 3 components: Total estimated revenue at the Qualified sales stage, Total revenue closed, and the length of time for an opportunity to move from the qualified stage to the closed stage. We use these components to build the following formulas.

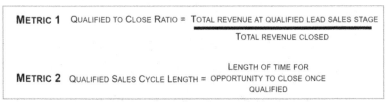

KEY REVENUE METRICS

Here is an example of how this works:

We can represent our sales cycle as a "funnel".

SALES PIPELINE

We have simply taken each sales stage and mapped it to a

funnel that represents the sales cycle starting with the leads at the top of the funnel, and ending with closed revenue at the bottom of the funnel. At each stage we assign a probability of the total revenue at that stage moving to the next stage. These probabilities are not random. They are determined by reviewing your actual results and then associating them to a percentage. As a result, we see declining amounts of revenue at each stage of the sales funnel. Each stage of the funnel is assigned a revenue value based on the total estimated revenue from all opportunities at that stage. As you can see from this example, you need $4M in total estimated revenue at the lead stage, to achieve $338K of closed revenue.

Once we know these numbers, we can start tracking our two key metrics. We can now apply them to calculate qualified to close ratio:

QUALIFIED TO CLOSE RATIO = *$338K / $1.5M (23%)*

We now know that approximately 23% of our revenue estimate at the "qualified" sales stage, will close. With this ratio calculated we can now estimate the closed revenue based on any amount of revenue at the qualified stage.

The next revenue metric is the qualified sales cycle length. As we mentioned before, it is not good enough to know your qualified closed ratio, you also have to know how long it takes for a qualified opportunity to move through the remaining sales cycle stages to closed revenue. The only way to calculate this value is to measure it. In our example, let's set this value to 90 days.

QUALIFIED SALES CYCLE LENGTH = *90 Days*

So what does this mean to your business. Well, if you are expecting to close $338K in revenue by March 31st, then you MUST have $1.5M revenue at the Qualified sales stage on January 1st. Now there is a chance that you might get the revenue by March 31st if you don't have $1.5M, but is is unlikely. Our goal is to drive predictable revenue, so we need to manage the numbers.

By understanding these two metrics, you can drastically impact your business. If you can increase your qualified to close ratio from 23% to 30%, then you will close $450K. How do you do this? Simply apply these methods you have read in this book. To get revenue faster, define your sales cycle and follow it.

Key Points

SALES IS A PROFESSION OF PROBABILITIES

KNOW YOUR REVENUE METRICS.

CONCLUSION

You can have the greatest offering in the world, but if someone won't give you money for it, then you don't have a business. Many great ideas never come to fruition because someone never quite figured out how to sell them. You now have the basics. It will take a lot more than simply reading this book. You will have to put these ideas into practice. Let's recap what you've learned.

The adage, "people buy from people they know and trust", is still as true today as it was 30 years ago. Make sure you have the trust mindset when you're selling your offering (Remember the Trust Cycle). You must have a sincere interest in helping your prospect. No gimmicks, tricks or manipulation. You must want to help them and if you can't, then tell them.

Don't be a "used car sales guy" who pitches his wares to everyone he meets. Make sure you get permission from your prospect to sell to them. How do you do that? You leverage your message to create curiosity. Curiosity will open the door to your conversation. This is the first step in the buyer's journey.

Leverage your message to get permission to have a sales conversation. Your message articulates your true business value in less than 10 seconds. It must be concise and to the point. It will open the door to prospects that are interested and close the door to those that are not interested. Your message will allow you to sell your value not your product or service.

Sales triggers in your message create buying signals from the prospect. It is the buying signal that gives you permission to start selling. Once you hear it, then you must get good at reading between the lines to understand what made the prospect truly interested in your offering.

Sales triggers create curiosity because they provide "glimpses of value" for the prospect who then becomes curious and wants to know more about how you can help them. This opens the door for you to begin asking questions that create credibility in the eyes of the prospect which in turn creates trust. As you ask questions that show you understand their german shepherds and gold medals, you become more credible and earn their trust. Of course, you must learn to shut up and listen.

Listening skills are crucial to successful conversations that produce sales. A successful conversation combines your knowledge of the prospect's business with the art of structuring a conversation that draws out urgency. Developing urgency is a must if you are going to create revenue for your business. Urgency is driven by emotion so don't be afraid to get emotional.

If you want your conversation to generate revenue, you must understand the next step. The next step is defined by your sales cycle. Make sure you follow it and not a random series of events defined by the prospect. So, know the next step and book a meeting from a meeting.

You are going to run into speedbumps along the road to closing a sale called objections. Remember that the objection you hear, may not be the real objection and use the objection formula.

STOP → LISTEN → CLARIFY → ANSWER

Finally, remember that sales is a profession of probabilities. You must play the odds and ensure that you have enough qualified opportunities to meet your revenue goals. To do this, you must manage your revenue metrics and know your ratios.

There you have it. A simple approach to sales. We hope you can see that generating sales is as simple as a conversation. It is just a series of successful conversations strung together with a purpose. The purpose is to develop trust, and results in your business growing its revenue. Anyone can do it, even you.

Key Points

YOU CAN'T SELL SOMETHING TO ANYONE UNTIL THEY GIVE YOU PERMISSION

DEVELOP A TRUST MINDSET TO BE SUCCESSFUL

SELL YOUR VALUE NOT YOUR PRODUCT

KNOW HOW TO ARTICULATE YOUR VALUE CONCISELY IN UNDER 10 SECONDS

SALES TRIGGERS CREATE BUYING SIGNALS

ALWAYS READ BETWEEN THE LINES

CURIOSITY STIMULATES INTEREST

GERMAN SHEPHERDS, GOLD MEDALS, AND FOLLOW THE HERD MOTIVATE PROSPECTS

STOP TALKING AND LISTEN, ALWAYS!

HAVE A CONVERSATION

Key Points

KNOW THEIR BUSINESS AND ASK CREDIBLE QUESTIONS

GET EMOTIONAL AND DEVELOP URGENCY, ALWAYS!

YOU CONTROL THE SALES CYCLE, NOT THE PROSPECT.

MANAGE THE STEPS - BOOK A MEETING FROM A MEETING (BAMFAM)

THE OBJECTION MAY NOT BE THE OBJECTION

STOP, LISTEN, CLARIFY, ANSWER!

SALES IS A PROFESSION OF PROBABILITIES

KNOW YOUR REVENUE METRICS

CONTROL THE CONVERSATION NOT THE PROSPECT

REFERENCES

Covey, S. (n.d.). *7 Habits of Highly Effective People.* Simon & Schuster.

Freese, T. (2013). *Secrets of Question Based Selling.* Sourcebooks.

ABOUT THE AUTHORS

FRANK DION

 Frank is a proven intrapreneur and entrepreneur executive with over 35 years of experience. From his humble beginnings with Xerox and where he progressed through the ranks to lead organizations at Savin Canada, Computerland Canada, and Toshiba. At each stage in his career he was hunted and hired as a revenue turnaround specialist. When sales were down and revenue was struggling, you hire Frank. He has received many awards for growing businesses. His strategic methodology that "SALES is a PROCESS not a PRODUCT nor a PERSON." Made his teams number one every time.

Tired of the corporate life and travel Frank decided to venture out on his own and started Acenetx Ltd an internet outsourcing company of many firsts. The first to bring TV to the internet, iCraveTV. The first company to broadcast a live rock concert on the internet. His partners were very intelligent engineers who pushed product and sales were slow. Then changing our process to value-based selling we rapidly grew our sales. The tested & true strategy of "Pitch Product and Survive or Sell Value and Thrive" worked again. After taking this company public Frank sold the company decided to change his focus and help entrepreneurs grow their business.

As he quickly realized with his own company, Frank knew that without revenue, any venture would fail. He packaged his approach to turning around companies and began consulting to the industry. Frank met Rob and the two combined their efforts under a new banner, Get More Sales Corporation, helping entrepreneurs pivot from pitching product to selling value. This led to the Sales Made Easy approach and the rest is history.

Frank lives in the Toronto, Canada area with his wife Barb. He has two grown children and 5 grandchildren. He is very much a family man and you can find him doting over the grandkids on weekends. During the week you may find him watching Netflix, but during the day, you will definitely find him focused helping entrepreneurs grow their revenue & margin.

ROBERT KINCH

Rob's history in sales, sales management and leadership spans 3 decades. He has built sales teams with fortune 500 companies at IBM and Microsoft. Starting in the technology distribution industry he sold himself to IBM where he progressed from entry level sales to leading North American teams within 5 years. While at IBM he was a key leader in the development of the worldwide software business partner channel and led the Canadian independent software vendor recruitment team and then a North American team. After great success and consistent overachievement, he took on the challenge of leading a North American mid-market sales team to 5 consecutive 100% clubs. He left IBM in 2007 to lead the medium business sales team at Microsoft, where he led the team to 4 consecutive years of 100% achievement.

In 2011, Rob left the security of a corporate job to become an entrepreneur. He launched a company to fill a need he recognized during his days in corporate North America – selling. He created a team of fractional sales executives and applied his methodology to drive new business for companies. He saw how many entrepreneurs were "flying by the seat of their pants" and were lacking in understanding the basics of sales.

During this time, Rob met Frank. Frank had been an entrepreneur for many years and had developed a strategic approach to sales for business. They found synergies in their approach and together they launched Get More Sales Corporation, where they help entrepreneurs pivot from selling their products to selling their value.

Rob lives in the Toronto, Canada area with his wife Anna-Lisa and 3 kids and 2 in-laws. He spends his time mentoring those who are willing, on success and entrepreneurship and of course selling. Rob enjoys writing and has written many articles, some of them published, some not. You can find his writing on the Get More Sales website at www.getmoresalescorp.com/news . When you don't find him writing he will be on the golf course thinking about what to write about next.

Made in the USA
Monee, IL
15 January 2020

20385897R10059